Discovering Your Universal Purpose

AUTHOR NAME

Elia Wani (Proffesa160)

ISBN-10: 198663082X
ISBN-13: 978-1986630825

DEDICATION

This book is dedicated to all people who want to discover their universal purpose and discover their true universal nature to unleash their full potential.

I am an inspirational speaker, project manager, digital marketer, comedian, actor, author, spiritual adviser and infinite being.

This is my second book after my first book:
Keys to mastery energy over flow.
On www.createspace.com select store in search bar and search title: Keys to mastery energy over flow
Or email: eliaproffesa13@yahoo.com and get a free copy of my first book: Keys to mastery energy over flow.

Thanks for reading!

CONTENTS

ACKNOWLEDGMENTS
Thanks for reading and support!

Author: Elia Wani (Proffesa160)

Business and feedback email:
eliaproffesa13@yahoo.com

Facebook personal page: Elia Wani

Facebook fan page: Proffesa160

Instagram: proffesa160

YouTube: proffesa160

CHAPTER 1. BEING FREE IS YOUR HIGHEST PURPOSE. BE EGOLESS, FIND THE UNIVERSAL SELF.

Do what you love but you are not what you do. Have a purpose that has positive impact on society and helps other people and yourself but you will always have more value than your purpose. Having a purpose is only important because your alive, being a live and discovering your true universal self is a purpose in its self. If your happy and free without a purpose than you can see the whole picture. Discover from your heart, from your true being what the universe or universal God wants you to do to live a good legacy when you leave this planet. When you ok that one day thousands of years from now you will be not be remembered but most people that you help and have had a positive impact when your alive will always remember you but even if they don't, you ok with it because you're not attached to outcome but you do what you love and you treat people fairly because you are doing things from the universal love and happiness within. Your just like the sun that shines and its energy sustains the earth but it does not expect something back. You become egoless because you doing what makes you truly happy from the universal love to serve others and the "me" gets out of the way and you start living from the all, the universal love, happiness, wisdom and universal God field like Jesus and Buddha etc. They forgot themselves and become one with the source and served from universal love and now the world cannot forget them. They served and helped others, shared their universal truth and more people are still following their teaching because their presence is still felt in the world 2000+ years after they left the world.

Surround yourself with people that see the greatness in you that you already see in yourself. When you distant from everything including the mind, body and the me, the ego. Then you are free to live from your true being, the universal awareness, consciousness, spirt and not from the person but from the true universal awareness, love and oneness within.

Do what put value and help others and yourself and the money will follow as a result but it is not the reason because you are doing from the universal love, peace and happiness within. Doing good and helping others becomes your nature. If you do what has a positive impact and helps 1 or 3 people or a millions of people it will not make a difference because you are doing from the true universal love within because you value the 1 or 3 people as the one million because your egoless but you share your gift with as many people as possible from the universal love within.

Learn to create your own opportunities so that you do not put all the control in someone else hands. You purpose is more than just work, start a family, retire and die but self-actualization and discovering your true universal nature will lead you to live life fully and happily from all angles. Live out your desires safely without harming yourself or other people so when you live this planet you not be a gosh that end up reincarnating because of unfinished business. But pay attention that you reach a point you have done most of what you love like traveling, hobbies, romance, spent time with family, meeting new people, entertainment etc. You notice your now repeating everything and you will not feel complete until discover from within that you are one with the source of everything, universal consciousness and awareness. Live as the universal awareness and your will find the source that is even greater than heaven and manifested everything. Then you will discover true joy and happiness that you will not attached to the things of this world, to the point you happy, content and blissful even when you are doing nothing then you free. Even the fear of death should go because you know you are eternal and universal because you **identify yourself as one with the source of life, universe, universal consciousness, awareness, spirit within which is the universal God that manifested everything in the universe. You're part of and one with the wordless source that even watches universal consciousness and manifested everything and is everything and beyond with no limit.**

It does not matter what you do but is it going to make you happy, is it going to leave you with good memories and does it have a positive impact on you and other people. Everyone has a different path but you will always find people of the same energy who are on your path. Do not spend your life living someone else life so that when you in your in your death bed you will be happy you lived the life you want and learnt from you mistakes and kept improving and growing. You will have no fear of death if you know you are the universal consciousness, awareness, love, unborn and wordless source that has to be released if you live from the heart and not the mind. Let your mind dissolve in your heart and universal consciousness, spirit of love and awareness within. Feeling universal and discovering you universal is the greatest feeling than anything in the world. **Your universal purpose is to feel and rest in your universal source and universal spirit, consciousness, awareness space within completely. Then you will know what to do will your time on earth because the spirit of the infinite universe or universal God will lead your way and you will be complete full of joy, love, bliss, happiness, contentment and abundance within that you never feel lack even when you are with no money like the universal God because you are now one with the source of life and everything.** Then You will start to be and to do what adds value to your life and other people in the world. You will start to do what helps others from your true universal self.

CHAPTER 2. YOU WILL ALWAYS HAVE MORE VALUE THAN YOUR PURPOSE

The rap musician Jay z once said, "if you have billions and billions of dollars and you're the only person on earth you will not enjoy the money you have." It is a good example for me to use to show that people give money value. Another spiritual teacher called Mooji once said, "if an entity from outer space came and said I will give you a billion dollars in exchange for your consciousness what would you say?". My answer is everyone would say no because without consciousness you cannot know you exist. So a human being will always have more value than their purpose and people give value to money because you part of the source, universal consciousness and awareness that manifest everything. More so you're not made for your purpose but your purpose is made for you. Like Jesus said man was not made for bible but the bible was made for man. If you do what you love and do what meets the needs of others and market it to them, the money will come. If you cannot find what course you love to study, job to do or how to start a business then go online on google or YouTube, read books, videos and talk to people that have your vision etc but come to your own conclusion. If you are not doing what your love because it did not work out then put the money you make to do what you love and also save for the future and invest in yourself, others and take advantage of opportunities that come in future to do what you love never give up on that. Write that book if your heart tells you, live your dreams, start that business, find that dream job, If you want to travel the world plan for it. Write and speech your truth if it motivates you and others. Do and study what you love. Give time to watch and listen to people that motivate you to be great. Keep discovering and do not settle until your find what you love to do to contribute to have a positive impact on yourself, society and the world. You will discover your purpose is more than just go to school, get a job or start a business, have a family, make money and die. Do not become the citizen of the mind or the world but discover that you're a universal citizen one with the source, universal consciousness, awareness and love that manifested everything and is everything. After you find the light you will value yourself, your family and people around you more. **When we discover the big** things about ourselves, we start to appreciate the small things. We start to release the source, infinite universe or universal God is taking care of us like giving us the ability to breath, eat, see, feel etc. The source has also given us the ability to take care of ourselves, family and the ability to use our talents and gifts to help benefit our selves, family, society and the world. The source uses the universal consciousness to speak for itself. King Solomon wrote in the bible, "we are gods" or we are gods one with the source and universal consciousness or universal God.

In other words we are the source and universal consciousness within the flesh. Like a wave in the ocean is the ocean. Accepting this will lead you to awaken to who you truly are.

CHAPTER 3. YOU ARE NOT THE BODY AND YOU ARE NOT YOUR MIND

It is important that we do not identify our self with the body and mind but instead identify yourself as the source and universal consciousness that if we pay attention to within us that observes and perceives what goes on in the body and mind etc. **Like a wave in the ocean is the ocean, You're the source that manifested everything because your one with the source if your aware and live as universal awareness, universal consciousness and not just a person, a feeling greater than heaven when you fully become it and fully awaken to the truth that you are the source and universal consciousness in the flesh**. It is the part of us the remains if you drop the body and mind. It is the part of us that observes and perceives everything and is not affected or touched by what goes on in our life or the world. **Some once asked me how do you distant yourself from the mind and body and this is what I replied:**
 Through meditation and deep breathing exercises a few minutes a day with eyes closed

in the beginning in a position your fully relaxed. Do not try to control your thoughts or mind but observe them and your body. Imagine your above your body and mind, emotions or thoughts traveling through the universe connected to everything around you until you feel from your heart the separation from body and mind cause your observing what's happening in your body and mind. With time even with eyes open you feel yourself observing your body and what's happening in your mind but key is to be the observer. Like you say I am who is saying that, so I am talking about the nonphysical part of us that observes everything happening in the mind and the body is who to identify yourself with to separate yourself from your body and mind so you do not identify yourself with what happens in the mind and body so you're in a position power, peace, joy, love, contentment, bliss and **universal oneness**. Associating with the body and mind leads to suffering, anger, hate, jealousy etc if things do not go your way.

To have universal peace, love and happiness. We should associate our self with part us that observe our body and mind, you will feel separate in time you feel pain cause you do not associate yourself with it and you do not associate yourself with what goes in your mind that leads to suffering. Whatever way you can use to realize you're not the body and mind use it. When you realize your true universal self that observes the body, mind and accept it as you and you will feel universal peace and feel the space, joy, contentment, love. Learn to be, rest and relax in your true being and pure self with no effort because it is who you really are. Every day with be more beautiful even when you're doing nothing because of the peace, happiness and universal love within. Let your mind become one with your heart, universal source of everything, universal spirit, consciousness and awareness within and you will find the timeless. You are the source and limitless. Become the awareness of who you truly are, one with the source or universal God. The infinite universe or universal God will protect you and give you the desires of your heart. And your reach to the point of being without desires but contentment because you burnt all your desires by resting and identifying yourself as the source watching your mind and body because desires come and go but the universal self, your true self remains untouched and content etc. What you think is your purpose comes and goes after you fulfill it but the timeless within you lives forever and that is your universal purpose is to be it and rest in it and everything else shall come to pass. Jesus called it the kingdom of God within you or spirit of God within. When you discover the spirit of the infinite universe within you will stop living from lack but by faith and living from the heart and your spirit. Discover yourself as the source, universal consciousness and not the mind and body. Everything that that you need to do in life will happen automatically. You will begin to realize you're not the only one in control but the source, universal consciousness, spirit and awareness of the universe is in control. Do you tell your body to digest your food, do you tell your body to get hungry but you feel hungry and you aware the body digest the food you eat. The some way you feel and perceive your true pure self, with your heart you will discover your spirit is one with the source, universal consciousness that manifested everything in the universe. Then your start doing everything from love. The body will die, what happens in your mind comes and go. Even memory fades but the awareness and consciousness within that is universal remains and the wordless source of everything is unborn and never dies, you're the source. This happens as a result of the third eye, crown, heart, cosmic and all unlimited chakras opening after you release **you are the universal self. We are universal and once you discover that you have found your way back home.**

CHAPTER 4. YOUR PURPOSE MAY ALWAYS BE CHANGING BUT YOUR UNIVERSAL SELF REMAINS THE SAME

As time goes we keep discovering what you are good at, saying you only have one purpose like to be a doctor, engineer etc, can be limiting. Keep discovering your Abilities do not limit yourself. Nelson Mandela was a lawyer but he also discovered he could become a politician and president that would help fight apartheid and racism in south Africa.

The point is every work that people do in society keeps the economy running even without cleaners most places and cities would have disease out breaks but people were not made for economy but the economy exist because of people. The rich are rich because people buy their products.

Martin Luther king Malcolm X were not afraid and were killed for fighting against mistreatment, killing and racism against black people in America and America has more people in Jail than China and they are mostly black people like the rap musician Tupac said. Tactics to prevent black people from developing etc and to reduce their population by making unfair laws that target blacks and by using police to kill innocent black people and get away with it. Nelson Mandela spent 25 years in prison and forgave those that put in prison and almost killed him during apartheid that America supported. China and Russia helped Africans to fight for independence so balance of power is very important than democracy used to push their agenda.

Africa should accept the challenge and aim to become the next Wakanda like in the movie black panther and develop their own way of government that leads to development, peace and progress etc.

Martin Luther king Malcolm X and Nelson Mandela they are people who discovered their true nature and universal love and spirit within so they were not afraid of death but doing what is right. People that understood that mistreating and killing other people because of hatred does not make you superior but means you are still under the influence of evil energy and evil entities that blind you from seeing you are in darkness and you do not see you are in energetic hell. They are a lot of people doing evil in the world thinking it's their purpose that include racism by mistreating and killing people of other races, tribalism by mistreating and killing people who are not their tribe, killing the innocent because their religion is different, stealing from others, murderers, rapist, corruption, causing wars, classism by mistreating the poor by making unfair laws etc. Their soul is in hell but they do not see it because they blinded by their evil ways and after they die their soul and spirit will end up in energetic hell where all the evil entities end up in the universe and they will feel the pain and suffering they caused because they love doing evil their soul and spirit will be in energetic hell until they learn their lesson and some will have to reborn until they find light and start doing good and pay their karma. Karma is another word for whatever you do shall be paid back to you good or bad by the universe or universal God. Like Jesus said what good is it if you gain the whole world but lose your soul. My brother Yong once what I thing is the best definition for sin, he said sin is anything you do that hurt other people and cause suffering to the world.

People who love to do good feel the weight and pain if they do something wrong and they ask for forgiveness from the universe or universal God and pay for their Karma by doing good. They stay away from doing evil because they feel karma that whatever they do will be paid back to them by the universe or universal God and source that manifest everything and is everything. Because they love to do good because they are living from the universal love within. People that discover they are the universal love, consciousness, awareness within will be in heaven on earth if they are aware they one with the source and live as that awareness. They will even find that which is greater than heaven if they are aware they are the source, universal consciousness, love and awareness within when they are still alive on earth and live as that awareness. After they die their soul and spirit will go to back to the source that is greater than the highest heaven and they become one with the source of everything, universal God or consciousness, spirit and universal love that manifested everything forever because they have the same energy of love and fairness. For their have graduated from the earth school, experienced what they needed to experience and they have released and are aware that nothing is more in the world and the universe then being one with the source then they will become the source and they will not reincarnate or they will not be reborn. Like attract like.

CHAPTER 5. LEARN FROM YOUR MISTAKES, FAILURES AND SUCCESS

Learning from you mistakes and failures makes you wiser. When you make a mistake you learn from it, forgive yourself and correct it. You understand that you are not perfect but the timeless within is. Use everything that happens to discover you true self and you reach spiritual maturity and you will go from believe to being and living from the universal love within.

They say the difference between the master and student is that the master has failed more than student.
The different between a successful business people and those that are starting a business is that they have made more mistakes, they do know that if you learn from your mistake now you learn to avoid it in the future.
 People that are more peaceful, joyful and happy full of universal love, have made the mistake of thinking they are the body and the mind that lead to suffering and pain that forced them to drop the body and mind and identify themselves with the source, spirit and universal consciousness within that observes everything including the mind, body, joy, love, happiness,

bliss etc. People who are working in or studying what they love have work worked in a job they hate and studied and passed a course because they only thought about money and not their interest.

People who are in relationship with someone they connect with the same energy and frequency have tried to dated people they had no connection with and it was not a good experience but they use that experience to appreciate the people of the same energy that they connect with and people that love them for who they are more.

This applies to everything you will always meet people of the same energy and frequency from all over the world. Those are the people you should surround yourself with to grow. People you do not connect with and are of different energy prepare the way for you to recognize those that are on your energy and frequency when you share ideas and it is like you already know and trust each other than people you may have known for long but you do not connect or are not yet on the same frequency.

Like the prostitute that blessed Jesus feet with oil was on same energy with Jesus so he accepted her to bless him because Jesus words and presence helped her to release she can be and do greater things than being a prostitute after she waken to her universal self because she felt the universal love because Jesus was one with the source or universal God. Her heart was open and she knew Jesus more than the disciples who thought Jesus should not talk to her because of what she did in the past but they were not aware of who she was in the present. She more spiritual awake in the present than them. Jesus told them, you never blessed my feet with expensive oil or you have not release yourself like her yet or you would have felt and known she has awaken to her universal consciousness, love and awareness of the source of life and everything.

People who know what it is like to be broke know the importance of saving for the future.

People who have missed investment opportunities learn to take advantage of future investment.
 People who have lost money from bad investment learn to invest with money they can afford to lose and let it grow and they have learnt how to take calculated risk.

The list goes on and on. Learn from your

mistakes what not to do to avoid making the same mistake next time and keep improving.

Learn from your success what to do to repeat your success and to keep improving and winning.

Be open to keep learning and improving in all areas of life.

CHAPTER 5. YOUR LIFE, OTHERS WAYS TO AWAKEN TO YOUR UNIVERSAL SELF AND PURPOSE

You do not have to live life because your life. You're the source and universal consciousness within that watches everything that happens.

Everyone has a different path to the truth and those are just a few ways but there are unlimited ways to have a spiritual wakening and becoming enlightened.

- It can just happen by universal grace, like for me I did nothing and had a spiritual awakening and I had to go online on YouTube and google to find out what was happening. I had no Idea it was a spiritual awakening so I had be open to learn from everyone who has found the spiritual truth.
- Meditation and deep breathing exercises up to the bottom of your stomach or spine when you have time every day can awaken the kundalini energy and open the third eye etc.
- Reading spiritual text, watching spiritual

videos that help you to discover, rest and experience your universal self and nature will help open the crown chakra, cosmic chakras and activate merkaba after all your chakras are open.

- When you heart chakra for love open, third eye for connection to spiritual world etc opens, throat for speaking your truth opens, crown for wisdom and cosmic connection etc opens, root for grounding opens with continual meditation deep breathing to the bottom of your stomach, and rest in the truth that your universal within, the rest of the chakras in between will open, including your cosmic chakras etc will also open.

- Control the sexual energy by no sex, no masturbation, no edging, no porn, for at least 3 days or more as you read wisdom, knowledge and watch videos to discover your universal nature and enlightenment.

- Living a healthy lifestyle by no drinking alcohol, no smoking cigarettes, no drugs and taking care of yourself. Exercise go for walks in nature or park, sun gazing when safe, eating a balance diet when following the spiritual path. The natural way is the best way.

- If you cannot stop drinking alcohol and smoking cigarettes etc. learn to take breaks from it. Too much of anything is bad but it is best to drop the habits if you can.
- Safe sex with twin flame or with someone you are connected to with same energy and frequency. This has no guarantee but awakening happen for some people this way.
- Sharing spiritual knowledge, wisdom and ideas with people who are on your same energy and frequency. Reading blogs, books and watching videos of people who are on the same path, frequency and energy of universal wisdom, love, consciousness and awareness.
- After a mother or a father has a child according to some people on the spiritual path.
- There are many others ways with grace the universe with help you become aware and find your way back home to the universal source of life within you. As above as below. As around you as within. Know thyself.

CHAPTER 6. TAKE ACTION TO GO TO THE NEXT LEVEL. MAKE YOUR NEXT MOVE YOUR BEST MOVE

Take action to meditate. Take action to discover your universal nature.

Take action to study what you love whether it is a certificate, diploma, degree or PhD what matters is that does it give you the information to work for yourself and others. Experience is the best teacher. Bill Gates, Steve Jobs and owner of Facebook are billionaires but they never finished university but they were doing instead of just studying. They discovered it is more important to have the mindset of the person who create PHD then to have a PHD. Instead of just working for others they opened their mind and discovered they could start their own company and put it into action and become the CEO or their own boss.

Learn to be a creator of ideas, products, businesses etc that changes your live and the life of other people in the world. Take action to create that business and become your own boss. Even if you are working for some else in your free time take time work on your own business ideas. Keep creating instead of just watching television and being online.

As a kid at the age of 8 with my 10 and 12 year old brothers Manasi and Yong with the help of big cousin brothers Modi and John in Africa we started our own small business selling different products and we were the only newspapers distributors in the village. It was our business we were all our own bosses and never worried about being fired but did was best for the business because it was our own. That is when I had a test of working for yourself with your own schedule too much freedom and money was no problem until we left the village and moved to Kampala city in Uganda. I am in Australia now and I am working on different online business ideas like my old brother Yong.

Take action to save money for future. For emergency, peace of mind and investment etc.

Take action to do what you love.
Take action to rest and take action to go on holiday, work without balance leads to break down.
Take action to travel.

Take action to make your dreams a reality etc.

This going be a short chapter straight to the point. Without taking action you will not know the result and learn from it. Even the bible says faith with no action is dead. **Take action to do what you love to day**. Take action to do what will take you to the next level. **Dreams and great ideas without action are dead.**

CHAPTER 8. HOW AFRICANS WHO DISCOVERED THEIR UNIVERSAL SELF, PURPOSE AND POWER STARTED CIVILIZATION IN THE WORLD

One of the story behind the black super hero Black Panther movie show mystical country Wakanda as the most advanced in the world and black panther as the richest super hero like Mansa Musa African king of Mali west Africa who was the richest man to ever live with personal wealth of 400 billion other people say trillion!. The movie also reflected many great African civilizations like.

The ancient black Egyptians and black pharaohs and black Africans in the Nile valley discovered their universal self, purpose came together and build, manifested the first great civilization in the world and build great cities, advanced medicine, agriculture, writing, build the pyramids, discovered their super powers etc. Knowledge and wisdom that started civilization in the world. Their kingdoms fall after 10,000 years and their descendants spread to other parts of African and left Ancient Egypt because of invasion by Europeans and Arabs etc. The

Europeans, Arabs and other invaders tried to cover up so they claim themselves as the builders if the pyramids but failed because Africans know their History and during the building of pyramids people where black in the region with different shades of black form dark to light skin with different furthers Africa is diverse before other people invaded or visited. The black pharaohs left behind so many statues to show they were black Africans from dark to light skin, writings and art with their African culture etc. they called themselves people of the sun only black people called themselves that. Their descendants moved to other parts of Africa because if invasions from, Europeans Arabs etc. No Arabs, Europeans etc call themselves people of the sun. This only important for Africans to accept that the ancient Egyptian where black Africans and let other people lie to themselves.

When you feel greatness within then you then you will discover your great talents. Main reason for this story is the Europeans etc who tried to cover the story knew the power if black people around the world discover their great history because that would lead to an awakening.

Africans had go back to their African culture

which included discovering their super powers and universal nature to disappear, turn in to lions etc that cannot be seen, disappear and go to other dimensions, make it rain like my great grandfather Yengi, grandfather Godi and uncle Pitia. These powers helped Africans to fight for independence and win the European colonialist.

My great grandfather Yengi was very powerful in Sudan he was a king descendant of black pharaohs of ancient Egypt that spread around African after invasion by out siders. The British put him in jail because he was powerful but other Africans told the British if you kill this man there will be no rain in this part of the country and those that killed him will die from the curse of his spirit he is lord of the land. The British asked him to make it rain so he made it rain for seven days and they begged him to stop the rain because of floods then he stopped it. He closed and opened his hand they could see lions, tigers etc moving in his hand. The British let him go and were afraid to kill him because he would come back in the spirit stop the rain and the curse of his spirit would kill those that killed him like the murderers who died after he cursed them for the murder of the innocent.

Europeans colonizes called African culture evil so they take the land after African lose their connection to the spiritual. The Chinese and Russians told Africans they gave you the bible misinterpreted so you lose your powers so they can take the land. That is why the black ancient Egyptians have a saying know thyself that is important for all humans being, so that your eyes are open and you will be easily deceived. Africans used their super powers by discovering their universal abilities and guns to fight and defeat the European colonialist.

Black Africans from the Nile valley came together to build ancient Egypt they had their time and stated the most advance civilization starting building pyramids, cities, temples, writing, medicine, agriculture, discovering their super natural abilities and super powers etc. Their Knowledge and wisdom that spread around the world. Then Europe used that knowledge to get out the dark ages and developed ahead but used their power to colonize other countries when it was their time and they lost the trust of other nations.
Now if see the top fastest growing countries the top 10 are in Asian and Africa so the world is shifting. Power is not a right but privilege. No

one knows which country and region will be the next world super power in the world in the next 10,000 years. But good leaders care about their people, development, peace, progress etc and they do what will leave a good legacy in the world.

Every country has a different system they should discover that will lead to peace, development and economic stability etc.

Prosperity for all should be the goal for the future so the world will move to the next level in the next 10,000 years.

Division because of race, tribe, region, class etc are used to benefit a few. Human being on earth have a long way to go. We should not base being superior because you oppress others and make unfair laws etc those are characteristics of being still barbaric, satanic and evil. Being superior should mean we now see that will are all equal with different gifts. We are all the human race one with the source, universal consciousness, love, awareness that manifested everything. Being superior should mean we want best for us and the world or we not better than the animals.

Not everyone and leaders in the world will

want to do what is good for all but when most people and leaders in the world want the best for themselves, others and the world regardless of race, gender, tribe, religion, class, region etc and realize we are all the human race then the world will go to next level of peace, prosperity etc. Then human beings will be a step ahead of the animals.

The world will be a better place in future if the good people fight for justice for all and use their voice to talk against injustice in the world.

Africa and upcoming countries have to realize they will have to be solve their problems and develop and do trade with one another to the point they do not need the west then they will have be able to negotiate better trade deals than the trader deals that favor and exploit African and upcoming countries natural resources etc. And if leaders who have experience, not perfect but have experience fighting colonialist and know their tactics. Like Rwanda is the second fasting growing country in the world and had elections but they call president Kagame a dictator but he won the elections by 96%, they say it is not possible but most people support him. Rwanda is the second fastest growing country in the world after china they are proud of their leader. Trump lost by 3 million votes to Hilary Clinton in American elections but still won. Do they call Australian prime minister or European countries with no term limits dictators no or Trump who won but Hilary has 3 million votes than him clearly not a perfect democracy if was another third world country with oil and natural resources they would call him a dictator and even invade it to control their oil and natural resources. Dictator by the west media is another word for leaders with influence the west has problems controlling and if they invade they make sure the leaders they cannot control with influence are killed like Gadhafi and Saddam. They have no problem with Saudi Arabia with one of the world largest oil reserves where women were not allowed to drive because the king is under their control and they control the oil.

Good performance and people support should determine how long a leader should stay in power. Every developing country should develop a system that leads to stability, peace, prosperity and opportunities that the average person can enjoy but a country should not be destroyed like Libya etc because some few people want to president. A country should not be destroyed to force a western style of government who are just after oil, natural resources, power and control and more influence etc than their opponents like China and Russia and do not care people are killed because their countries are peaceful and developed. Great leaders like president Kagame of Rwanda, Putin of Russia etc are rare and should be given time to stabilize and develop their countries. Every country is different and should be given time to develop a system that work for them for them to stabilize the economy, have peace and development. Not just put a western system of government and change leaders like underwear even if they good like Kagame for the west to benefit because they are put by them like in Libya and Iraq etc. It is indirect colonization. The people suffer and many killed. All the west care is their political interest because they want control over other developing countries.

CHAPTER 9. OVERCOMING THE OBSTACLES TO DISCOVER YOUR GREATNESS

Jesus, Buddha etc discovered their universal nature within and become one with the source and are membered to this day. Instead of worshiping them let them inspire you to also discover your universal self and nature and you will graduate from believe to being because your experiencing oneness with the universal source of life and everything.

Everyone has a different path.
The mind and people who are not free do not want you to be free and others only want themselves to have this knowledge especially the elite etc. Science is now catching up with quantum physic etc. When it comes to spiritual things talk to those that are experiencing it and find people you connect with the same energy and frequency.
Science will always be behind because the powers that be know many people are waiting for scientist to approval to accept this truth so they will pay them to lie to the public. But let scientist do scientific things and let the

spiritually aware people talk about what is spiritual. Do you want to know your spiritual universal self from a scientist that will call you crazy or the spiritual people you connect with. I listen to people that can make it rain, disappear etc like my grandfather's King Yengi and Godi and uncle Pitia that have died but are there in the spirit or other spiritual teaches and people I connect with.

I am also grateful to have a family that is spiritual. My Dad Samuel Udu helped me to get a better tittle that helped me write this book. I was going to call this book discovering your universal self but dad was like discovering your universal purpose will be more powerful. So I took his advice. It is always good to ask and talk to the right people.

So speak to the specialist. Leaving a healthy life has helped me discover my universal self and purpose more. I used to drink alcohol, smoke, cigarettes. I used to also smoke weed once in few months it awaken my kundalini and opened my third every, crown but I was not grounded I felt on top of the world full of love, peace and universal oneness but ended in psychiatrist hospital they told me I had bipolar because I could not stop talking and because I told them I was from a royal family. I told them spiritual concepts they instead said you are crazy but their medication never worked well and made me not fully feel my emotions. But a spiritual psychologist asked to talk to me when I was locked in the psychiatric hospital because I was ungrounded, could not stop talking, could not sleep well and was full of energy, he was white but his wife was African from a different royal family like me too. He had been to African countries like Uganda etc where I was born. He told me after listening to me that your spiritually awake and intelligent. My wife is also from a royal African family like you she told me in Africa most tribes have a Kings and chiefs. I heard the nurses and chief psychiatrist call you crazy for saying you a prince from a royal family but I told them African countries have many royal families. I told him almost every tribe and he said yes they have no idea but I do. I told him my Dad told me that even chiefs are Kings but the British and Europeans called them chiefs to down grade them to make their kings and queens in Europe feel better. He understood me because he knew African spiritual culture, history and he was on the same frequency, had the same good energy and the same spiritual knowledge/wisdom like me. Even before talking to him I told him you have very good energy. He told me you cannot stop talking because of anxiety you full of energy you do not have bipolar. After hospitalization my brother Yong, sister Mary told my dad Samuel about natural herbs after I was locked in a psychiatric hospital for 30 days without seeing the sun a number of times. I started taking natural herbs for anxiety to balance my energy and now I take natural herbal magnesium and Siberian ginseng after trying other herbs for anxiety. I had to stop drinking and smoking, no weed, no drugs. I tried to tell my psychiatrist after I was out of hospital that I am only taking natural herbs and she almost put me back in hospital saying I have bipolar and anxiety but I only listened to the psychologist who said I only have anxiety that made me to not stop talking and be hospitalized many times because the bipolar medication could not stop me from talking nonstop. So I deceived them saying I take their psychiatrist medication for bipolar and anxiety that had bad sign effects and I could not function, injection in the past where worse so they stopped them after I told the review panel. The chief psychiatrist told me your IQ is above average after I challenged him because I was reading his mind and felt what he may said next and I also had done my own research to discover I was going through a spiritual wakening online on YouTube and google etc. I deceived them that I was taking their psychiatrist medication and my family kept the secret too. Until I was so well from the natural herbs they told me to stop seeing them after I told them I was well I did not want to see a psychiatrist. They told me to stop seeing them after months following up after I told them I am good on my own. The drinking, smoking cigarettes, weed made me ungrounded. The natural way to spiritual wakening is the best. I had to listen to my body to live a healthy lifestyle.

The best way is eating a balance die, meditation, self-inquiry and talking time to control my sexual energy no sex or porn or musturbation for 2, 3 days or more to help to raise the kundalini energy. But knowing I am the source and universal consciousness within and experiencing the oneness with the infinite universe and the source of everything has defeated my mind to become one with my heart. When my mind become one with the heart, source, universal consciousness, love, joy, bliss within. The mind and everything when to zero and no noise I can feel the peace within all the time.

My eyes opened when my sister Mary and

brother Manasi told me, you are reading our minds. My sister told me the chief psychiatrist in the past was careful when they talk to you and review panel because you were reading their mind and felt what they will say next.

One of the tactics used by governments in the west and the world is by calling people who have a spiritual awakening and become ungrounded bipolar, crazy etc because they can cause a revolution like Martin Luther king etc. it is called the fear of the next messiah. Then they put them on chemical medications that destroy their energy and close the third eye, crown etc. When they would okay be if they could stop drinking, smoking and doing drugs including weed or take natural herbs, crystals to ground them or learn to meditate and balance their energy.

.

There are people who their brain and mind is damaged and take psychiatric medication and it works for them, we are all different. If one crazy person does thing stupid. They want to put every one they think is crazy in the same category which wrong but everyone is responsible for their action. Back in Uganda in Africa the homeless crazy people are judged according to their actions and not the actions of other crazy people just like everybody else so they feel accepted and very few commit suicide even without medication. There is no need to take any medication that you do not need and natural herbs can work but are only taken when necessary. The pharmaceutical companies, their psychiatrists and doctors etc will never say natural herbs work better for some people than their chemical medication when treating any problem or sickness because they lose profits.

When you start to accept you not the mind, body, you're not the future, past or present etc. But you're the universal consciousness, awareness and the wordless source that even watches consciousness within that is limitless and manifested everything and is everything because you are experiencing it the duality will go. Then You will live from the source and the source or universal God will lead your way. The body will get sick, your thoughts in your mind, emotions come and go, problems come and go, you may take medication etc but you know you are the source and universal spirit within that observe and perceive everything that remain untouched and you be free if you experience and identify with that within you that is the effortless pure self, being that words cannot

not describe but you feel it in your heart, soul and spirit then nothing will take you away your freedom and liberation.

Even after the body drops and dies you remain. You're one with the source, unborn, limitless, universal consciousness, awareness, universal God and wordless that even watches consciousness. Rest and find peace in it and the I am moves out of the way and you start to live from the all. And from the all you will manifest what will be of value to you, family and other people in the world. From the all you are above your problems like an eagle that fly's above the storm when are birds are try to hide but cannot because they are in the storm. The storm is the mind. If you above the mind, you are aware your problems come and go and you will not associate yourself with your problems but naturally solve them.

CHAPTER 10. DISCOVERING TRUE SUCCESS, WHAT MATTERS IN THE END?

True success is discovering you are the universal consciousness within that observes everything. Then everything you do will be a reflection of the greatness you feel within.

Steve Jobs who created Apple but was once homeless but he never gave up on his ideas and gifts and changed the world. Elon Musk the founder of Tesla that make electric cars and SpaceX started his own company PayPal before he sold it because he could not find a job at computer companies and he repeated his success by starting Tesla and SpaceX. Lisa Nicolas of the secret once said the billionaires and millionaires teach me how to make money and some of them pay me to teach them the spiritual secrets.

To me equally successful are those have discovered they are the source that manifested everything in the universe within

the flesh.

My childhood story

I was in gun point in 1993 in north Uganda with my parents and brother Manasi. My dad Pastor Samuel Udu was the chairman of all Pentecostal churches in Sudan and the charity he headed gave clothes to 5000 people in Northern Uganda refugee camps and to local villagers but the other Sudanese people wanted his position because he was not corrupt so they hired gunmen to kill my parents and us who were witnesses. The gunman pointed the gun at me I was 5 years and brother 7 years old and the other gun man said leave them they are angels. The energy in the room was high it started to rain, help from the ancestors and universal God or universe. They were going to shot but my mom and she sensed it before they could shot and she pushed herself and my father forward so they do not have a clean shot so their blood flash on them and if they run other villages will know they shot someone because my parent were next to the wall in the grass thatched house but when my parents moved forward their high energy freeze the gunmen and they ran outside.

The female warriors in the movie black panther

movie reminded movie me and my Dad of my Mom Jeselina Kiden. They about to shot but mom was not afraid to speak up push forward and the energy freeze the gun men and they run out side they ask Dad to come out side so they shot him but dad challenge them to come in. Dad was said it was like in black panther movie let the challenge begin part.

My brother Chaplain came out of nowhere saw the gunmen and ran and yelled to warn the people in other houses that there gunmen, the gunmen shot but missed my brother the bullet went through the door and missed my other cousins and brothers. They come back and tried to take my dad to shot him but he lied he was coming to join them and run away to the bush they could not see him because it was dark. They got afraid my brother and father may call other villagers to come and arrest them and they ran away it rained the whole night than before. The next day we moved to a new city. That was the day I realise the universe or universal God is powerful. The universe, high energy and nature the rain and darkness protected us. If you have a good heart the source the universe will protect you. By the grace of universe and universal God n mom etc. we still here alive in 2018.

Glad people liked my first book and asked me to write another one. Thank you for reading!!!

Conclusion
I am the last of ten children I was born on the 25th December 1987 in the bush deep in the bush a free land given to refugees in Uganda in refugee camp in Northern Uganda near the river Nile after my family ran from Sudan (now South Sudan) to Uganda because of the war when my mom was pregnant with me. My dad and mom are from South Sudan, my mom's father was Ethiopian so people from Sudan are no sure I am Sudanese because I am not black enough and some Ethiopian are not sure I am Ethiopian because I not light skin enough but some Africans think I am Kenyan, others think I am Nigerian or think am from Zimbabwe etc but I was born in Uganda. Ugandans think I am Uganda until I start to talk and sound different, Australian ask me do you like it here? on a hot sunny day. I never been to South Sudan or Ethiopia yet so I have never been in country that I can call my country but who created this borders it is all one world and we are all the human race on earth for a short time. So I decided to call myself I a **universal citizen** because no one will say that is my country the

universe. That is when I felt finally home. Knowing is not enough aim to experience your true **universal oneness**, home, the source and drop all identities.

feel your absolute, pure, timeless alone existence and you will release you are never alone you are one with the source then you will never be lonely but always whole. Feel and be the unbroken existence within that shines by its self. Feel and experience the wordless, space, oneness, presence, love, freedom, and universal consciousness within. I came to realise this because I spent most of my 30 years alone because I always feel I was not alone now I know why. Feels good to discover the true home within.

You may not understand this book until your fully waken but the fact that your reading this book means you have found your way to experience the universal oneness or you are on your journey to but realised there was no journey in first place you are what you are looking for....

You are the source and universal consciousness within the flesh.

Thank you for reading and for your support! May the universe bless you. May the grace of the source, infinite universe or universal God lead your way to discover the source, greatness, peace, love, and universal consciousness within.

AUTHOR: Elia Wani

Discovering your universal purpose

ABOUT THE AUTHOR

I am an inspirational speaker, project manager, digital marketer, comedian, author, spiritual adviser and infinite being.

Elia Wani (proffesa160)

Business and feedback email: eliaproffesa13@yahoo.com

Facebook personal page: Elia Wani

Facebook fan page: proffesa160

Instagram: proffesa160

YouTube: proffesa160

Made in the USA
Columbia, SC
25 July 2021